365 THOUGHTS
OF PEACE AND HOPE

WHITE STAR PUBLISHERS

365 THOUGHTS
OF PEACE AND HOPE

CONTENTS

SOLID BRICKS FOR BUILDING PEACE

LIST OF CONTRIBUTORS - PHOTO CREDITS

SOLID BRICKS FOR

Words are a continuous flow of varied sounds and signs, always present in our lives as individuals, as groups and communities, and for mankind as a whole. If we imagine a world without words, we see one without any communication, isolated and desolate.

Appearing first in the mind, then flowing from the mouth or the pen (these days perhaps from the computer keyboard or the keys of a cell phone), words enable us to communicate with each other, to express our feelings, cultivate human relationships, express ideas, defend principles, or even simply sing a favorite song.

When looked at more closely, however, words are essentially neutral; their effect depends on the intentions of those who use them. Words do not always imply a shared sense of right and wrong, in-depth analysis or mature reflection. In some situations a word may be misused, so that it becomes a trap, creating misunderstandings for the individual or the group, and, in the worst case, becoming a dangerous weapon that can trigger or encourage wars.

So it is that a word is something that in practical terms may push the world towards good or evil, according to how it is used.

For this precise reason and today more than ever it is vital to reflect on famous phrases, expressions and words (or rather those expressed by well-known people in historically significant contexts) that are universally understood, so as to ignite and keep alive a light visible to all regardless of geographical, ethnic or cultural context. Rich in positive messages and able to echo powerfully in

BUILDING PEACE

the collective imagination, words can form useful points of reference that on a moral level are both abstract and concrete for a humanity that is often adrift and confused by uncontrollable events of global concern. Thus, in moments of extreme difficulty when the view of life itself seems blurred, words offer a safe haven for those who have lost their way and stopped facing the future. Words of wisdom, intelligent, forward-looking words that have won the battle against time by enduring until our own day, words that are destined to continue shining for who knows how much longer.

The great minds that have fueled progress, the outstanding characters whose works and deeds have benefited the entire world, the philosophers and religious figures who have encouraged the cultivation of harmony, solidarity, and integration among peoples, have always represented a timeless foundation for humanity everywhere. The speeches of artists and enlightened heads of state, the aphorisms of great people of the past, philosophers, men and women of faith, writers and poets, and peace activists, can become sources of inspiration, instilling vital confidence, stimulating reflection, and helping us cultivate the conscience of a united humanity.

So, when animated by constructive intentions that are benevolent and based on respect for others, words stimulate individuals to plant the seeds of a harmony that can continue to grow and spread in their daily lives. Such words are a powerful means of conveying information that can influence the destiny of the world, helping people prepare for the realities of life in a balanced way.

More specifically, they represent the best way of nourishing that sentiment that enables people to face problems and survive the darkest times: hope.

It is precisely hope that, even in the most extreme and dramatic situations, enables people to be reconciled to life and open themselves to the future with optimism.

In a time of great contradiction and uncertainty such as the present, the hope shared by everyone is first and foremost the hope for peace. A desire that grows more intense every day and requires constant individual and collective effort if a stable global situation is to be achieved. Since antiquity, a desire for peace, the natural predisposition of the human creature, a spontaneous desire, the supreme ideal, has been a subject of the greatest interest to artists, philosophers and, of course, rulers and politicians of all cultures.

Over the centuries, the quest for peace has counteracted movements of oppression and violence designed to disrupt the equilibrium between individuals or nations. Many have worked with words to achieve, maintain, and defend peace, to spread culture and to dismiss the shadow of devastating conflicts. From Ghandi, the extraordinary idealist of non-violence, to Martin Luther King, symbol of the struggle against racial segregation, from John Fitzgerald Kennedy, the unforgettable 35th President of the United States, to Nelson Mandela, one of the most admirable examples of the fight against racism, numerous prominent individuals have spoken in favor of a peace and serenity that would protect individuals and the entire human race in every corner of

the globe. And indeed it is also thanks to their words that humanity has al-
ways managed to overcome times of dejection and to recover from situations
that have severely put it to the test. Universal peace, then, but also (and per-
haps even primarily) the peace that is found in small gestures, in little things,
in events that concern each of us in our own everyday dimension. These mi-
croscopic aspects of the human condition may be disparagingly defined as in-
significant, but in fact form the essential basis of a much broader equilibrium,
even on a global scale.

There are many examples of behavior and events that have made the whole
world ponder, and that have often contributed conclusively to the containment
of hostilities, the avoidance of direct confrontation and, above all, to the spread
of the culture of peace: anti-war marches, the annual award of the Nobel Peace
Prize, the celebration of the World Day for Peace established by Pope Paul VI
in 1967, and unforgettable acts like those of the unknown insurgent who blocked
the tanks in Tiananmen Square in 1989. But in addition to all these things,
many great minds have courageously handed down a conceptual heritage of
immeasurable value: through their words, which have been indelibly carved
in history and, still today, represent brilliant beacons that will illuminate the
path of humanity, forever.

Gabriele Atripaldi

It is time to make peace
with the planet.

– *Al Gore*

JANUARY

2

January

No act of kindness, no matter
how small, is ever wasted.

– *Aesop*

3

January

No night or problem is able
to defeat dawn or hope.

– Bernard Arthur Owen Williams

4

January

Man may be free,
if he resolves to be so.

– Voltaire

5

January

Think peace, live peace and breathe
peace, and you'll get it as soon as you like.

– John Lennon

6

January

The only magic formula for bringing up
children is to give them plenty of love.

– Grace Kelly

7

January

I live on hope and so I think do all
who come into this world.

– Robert Seymour Bridges

8

January

Friendship is a single soul dwelling
in two bodies.

– Aristotle

9

January

The only thing we have to fear
is fear itself.

– Franklin Delano Roosevelt

10

January

I dream a world where all
will know sweet freedom's way.

– Langston Hughes

11

January

Inner peace is the ultimate source
of happiness, joyfulness.

– Tenzin Gyatso (Dalai Lama)

12

January

Love is a word of light,
written by a hand of light, upon a page of light.

– Kahlil Gibran

13

January

Real angels are those people who appear suddenly
in certain moments to bring light to our lives.

– Banana Yoshimoto

14
January

Start by doing what is necessary,
then what is possible,
and suddenly you are doing
the impossible.

– Saint Francis of Assisi

15
January

God has put a secret art
into the forces of Nature
so as to enable it to fashion itself
out of chaos into a perfect world system.

– Immanuel Kant

16

January

Brick walls are there for a reason.
They give us a chance
to show how badly
we want something.

– Randy Pausch

17

January

Can miles truly separate you
from friends… If you want to be
with someone you love, aren't you
already there?

– Richard Bach

18

January

Free man, you will always cherish the sea!

– Charles Baudelaire

19

January

Where no sea runs, the waters
of the heart push in their tides.

– Dylan Thomas

20

January

It gets dark sometimes, but morning
comes. ... Don't you surrender!

– Jesse Louis Jackson

21
January

If God is thy father,
man is thy brother.

– Alphonse de Lamartine

22
January

... and he saw his steps filled
with peace, he saw his head
surrounded by splendour,
he saw his body radiating with light.

– Hermann Hesse

23

January

... only those who dare may fly.

– Luis Sepúlveda

24

January

It doesn't matter if you're born in a duck yard,
so long as you are hatched from a swan's egg!

– Hans Christian Andersen

25
January

Paradise is not of this world
but there are some fragments.

– Anonymous

❧

26
January

Do you love life?
Then do not squander time;
for that's the stuff life is made of.

– Benjamin Franklin

27

January

Never measure the height of a mountain
until you have reached the top.
Then you will see how low it was.

– Dag Hammarskjöld

❧

28

January

Think of all the beauty that
is around you and be happy.

– Anna Frank

29
January

... light loses its blinding flash
and diffuses itself all around,
regenerating, peace ...

– Walt Whitman

30
January

I put dreams above everything else.
Reality is often a dream.

– Walter Bonatti

31

January

Your heart is a seagull that flies
freely in the sky of life.
Let it go without fear, it will know
how to lead you to happiness.

– *Sergio Bambarén*

1

February

Where flowers bloom,
so does hope.

– Claudia Alta "Lady Bird" Taylor Johnson

FEBRUARY

2

February

Do what you can, with what you have,
where you are.

– Theodore Roosevelt

3

February

Each one sees what he carries
in his heart.

– Johann Wolfgang von Goethe

4

February

We are all light bulbs.
If bliss starts growing inside you,
it's like a light;
it affects the environment.

– David Lynch

❧

5

February

The word is the light of humanity,
and light is the word of Nature ...

– Giovanni Battista Niccolini

6
February

Freedom in the mere sense
of independence is meaningless.
Perfect freedom lies
in the harmony of relationship
which we realize not through
knowing but in being.

– Rabindranath Tagore

7
February

You can't separate peace from
freedom because no one can be
at peace unless he has his freedom.

– Malcolm X

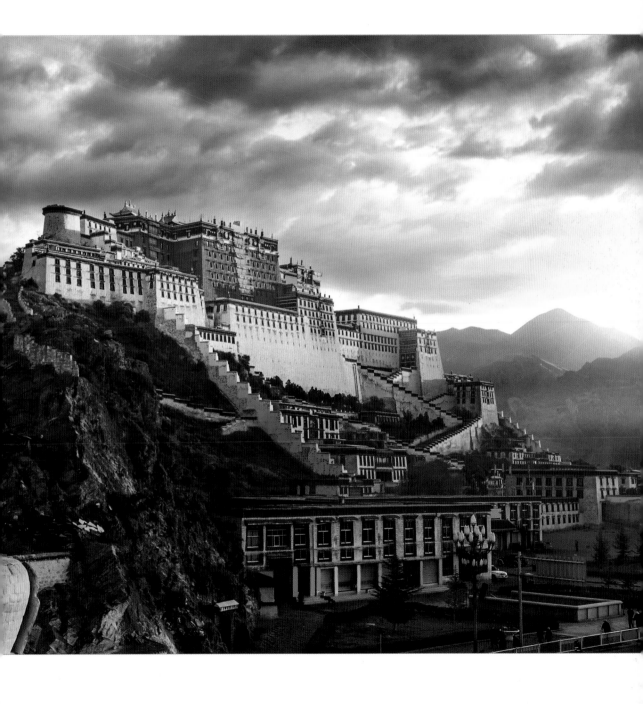

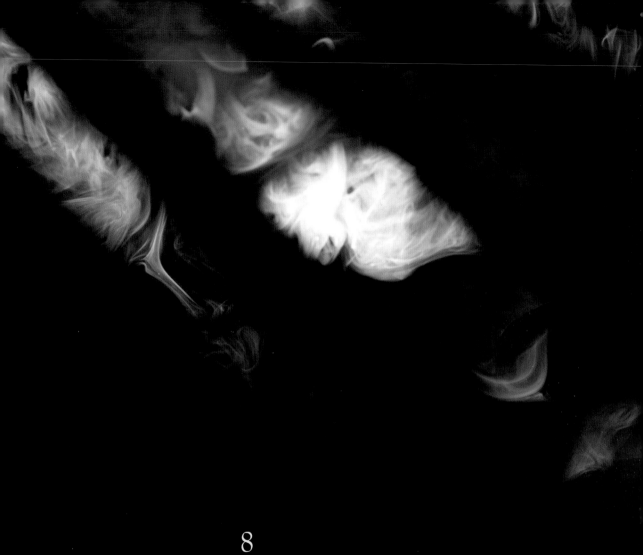

8

February

Our smile affirms our awareness and
determination to live in peace and joy.

– *Thich Nhat Hanh*

9
February

Limits exist only in the soul of those
who are short of dreams.

– Philippe Petit

10
February

All fantasy should have
a solid base in reality.

– Max Beerbohm

11

February

One must have dreams, and fight to make them come true.

– *Francesco Alberoni*

12

February

As long as you're going to be thinking anyway, think big.

– Donald Trump

13

February

... Liberty lends us her wings
and Hope guides us by her star.

– Charlotte Brontë

14

February

The privilege of a lifetime
is being who you are.

– Joseph Campbell

15

A single grateful thought toward
heaven is the most perfect prayer.

– Gotthold Ephraim Lessing

16

February

Do not be afraid. Darkness is never
quite as dark as we imagine it to be.

– John Osborne

17

February

... the fact that everybody in the world dreams
every night ties all mankind together ...

– Jack Kerouac

18

February

There is in the world only one way on
which nobody can go, except you: where
does it lead? Do not ask, go along with it.

– Friedrich Wilhelm Nietzsche

19
February

No, no, we are not satisfied
and will not be satisfied until justice
rolls down like water
and righteousness like
a mighty stream.

– Martin Luther King

20
February

Love has no limits. Love never ends.
Love is reborn and reborn
and reborn.

– Thich Nhat Hanh

21

February

Emancipate yourselves from mental slavery.
None but ourselves can free our minds.

– Bob Marley ("Redemption Song")

22

February

One right alone justifies
the creation of the world.

– Talmud

23

February

... I shook off difficulties,
like water on a duck's back.

– Rita Levi-Montalcini

❧

24

February

Peace is a never-ending process, the work of many
decisions by many people in many countries.

– Oscar Arias Sánchez

25
February

Friendship doubles our joy
and divides our grief.

– Francis Bacon

26
February

At the center of nonviolence stands
the principle of love.

– Martin Luther King

27
February

Beauty will save the world.

– Fyodor Mikhailovich Dostoyevsky

28/29
February

There is one spectacle grander than
the sea, that is the sky; there is one
spectacle grander than the sky,
that is the interior of the soul.

– Victor Hugo

Love is the force that transforms
and improves the Soul of the World.

– Paulo Coelho

MARCH

2

March

Because we all share
this small planet earth,
we have to learn to live
in harmony and peace with each
other and with nature.
That is not just a dream,
but a necessity.

– Tenzin Gyatso (Dalai Lama)

3
March

Hopefully we can grow a family that is infilled with hope, that is
inspired by stories, that uses its brain to further the generation of
young people who go out there and know that they make a difference.

– Jane Goodall

4
March

Courage is resistance to fear,
mastery of fear, not absence of fear.

– Mark Twain

5

March

For the establishment of peace
and human dignity,
each of us must work
and fight to the last.

– René Cassin

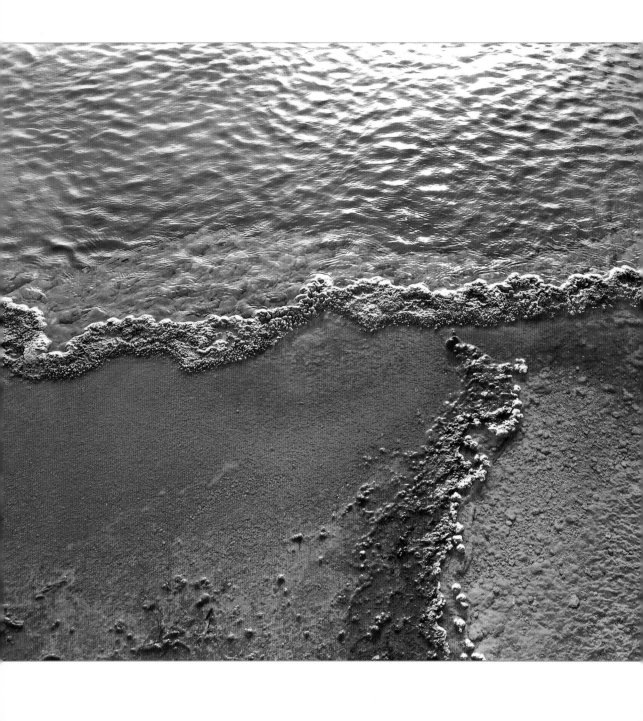

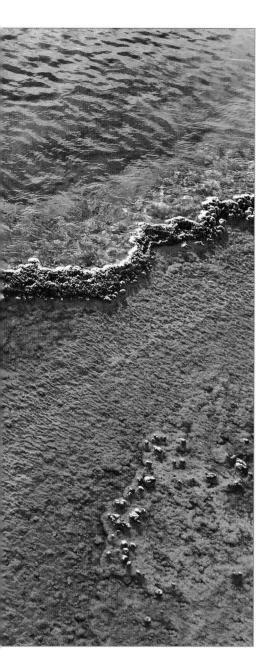

6

March

Every bliss achieved is a masterpiece ...

– *Marguerite Yourcenar*

7

March

Peace, progress, human rights - these three goals are insolubly linked to one another: it is impossible to achieve one of these goals if the other two are ignored.

– *Andrei Dmitrievich Sakharov*

8

March

The problem of war and peace
will be radically different the day
that women and men contribute equally
to the destiny of humankind.
Mothers and wives have only
one solution to this problem: peace.

– Sophia Loren

9

March

He sits watching the world as one may watch
a great play before the rise of the curtain.

– Abraham "Boolie" Yehoshua

10

March

Courage is the ladder on which
all the other virtues mount.

– Clare Boothe Luce

11

March

Then cherish pity, lest you drive
an angel from your door.

– William Blake

12

March

Trust in dreams, for in them is the
hidden gate to eternity.

– Kahlil Gibran

13
March

What counts among friends is not
what they say, but what you do
not need to say.

– Albert Camus

❧

14
March

No love, no friendship can cross the
path of our destiny without leaving
some mark on it forever.

– François Mauriac

15

March

If you are a free man then you are
ready for a walk.

– Henry David Thoreau

16

March

My best friend is the one
who brings out the best in me.

– Henry Ford

17
March

True friendship is made of trust,
loyalty and indulgence.

– Ralph Waldo Emerson

18
March

Of all the things which wisdom
provides to make us entirely happy,
much the greatest is the possession
of friendship.

– Epicurus

19
March

Do not seek yourself outside yourself.

– Aulus Persius Flaccus

❧

20
March

How I think one masters one's
life is to understand that you are
co-creating that life with
the ultimate Creator.

– Oprah Winfrey

❧

21
March

If you want to be happy, be so.

– Lev Nikolayevich Tolstoy

22
March

Only that which is real never changes ...

– Adi Shankara

23
March

... love is heaven and heaven is love.

– Walter Scott

24

March

Peace comes from being able to contribute the best
that we have, and all that we are, toward creating a world
that supports everyone.

– Hafsat Abiola

25

March

Man is a small ordered world.

– Democritus of Abdera

26

March

I want to live, not be a witness to my life.

– Jacqueline Lee Bouvier Kennedy

27

March

In the beautiful tomorrow
So much sweeter than today
In the beautiful tomorrow
Well tears will pass away
There'll be no heartache
And no pain
In the beautiful tomorrow
So much sweeter than today

– *Mahalia Jackson ("Beautiful Tomorrow")*

28
March

Be praised, my Lord, through all
Your creatures.

– Saint Francis of Assisi

29
March

I am the lord of my destiny,
the captain of my soul.

– William Ernest Henley

30

March

Light is internal, it lies inside of us ...

– Maxence Fermine

✵

31

March

No man who depends and relies
entirely on himself will be happy.

– Marcus Tullius Cicero

1

April

Friendship is
a sheltering tree.

– *Samuel Taylor Coleridge*

APRIL

2

April

Life is the flower for which
love is the honey.

– Victor Hugo

3

April

Variety's the very spice of life,
That gives it all its flavour.

– William Cowper

4

April

We spin many spider webs in the
emptiness to create the one
that will retain happiness.

– Augusta Amiel-Lapeyre

5

April

The heart resumes its role
as the source of the noblest virtues
that initiate pacific action:
Love, Initiative, Tenacity,
Realism, Patience.

– Dominique Pire

6

April

Whatever little we can do in our
own little corner makes a difference,
and collectively we take
a giant step forward.

– Kofi Annan

7

April

Man's main task in life is to give
birth to himself.

– Erich Fromm

8

April

Men and women are entrusted with the task of
crafting their own life, making of it a masterpiece.

– Pope John Paul II

9

April

[...] to look at the world in another way. To look at it in your own way, in the most sensitive way.

– Tiziano Terzani

10

April

I longed to arrest all the beauty that came before me,
and at length that longing has been satisfied.

– Julia Margaret Cameron

11

April

The proper function of man is to live, not to exist.
I shall not waste my days in trying to prolong them.
I shall use my time.

– Jack London

12

April

Happiness is not having what you want,
but wanting what you have.

– Oscar Wilde

13
April

Love emits colours in life.
Grey becomes a rainbow, it explodes
in a thousand colours, the monotonous
and the flat become psychedelic.

– Osho Rajneesh

14
April

Be thou the rainbow in the storms
of life. The evening beam that smiles
the clouds away, and tints tomorrow
with prophetic ray.

– George Gordon Noel Byron (Lord Byron)

15
April

"And when all the wars are done,"
I said, "a butterfly will still be beautiful."

– Ruskin Bond

16

April

I know one freedom and that
is the freedom of the mind.

– Antoine de Saint-Exupéry

17

April

Through nonviolence,
courage displaces fear.
Love transforms hate.

*– SNCC (Student Nonviolent Coordinating
Committee Statement of Purpose)*

18

April

Joy is the lifeblood of all human affairs.

– Pierre Bayle

19

April

Don't sacrifice your convictions for the
convenience of the hour.

– Edward Moore Kennedy

20
April

It's better to add life to your days
than days to your life.

– Rita Levi-Montalcini

21

April

Being understood means being taken
and accepted for what we are.

– Natalia Ginzburg

22

April

Don't compromise yourself.
You're all you've got.

– Janis Joplin

23
April

I have no home but me.

– Anne Truitt

❦

24
April

Research is not only useful
for what is being sought;
research includes the compensation
for its effort.

– Dacia Maraini

25

April

... he who has valour will always be
beautiful.

– *Sappho*

26
April

Nothing is difficult for those
who love.

– *Marcus Tullius Cicero*

27
April

Sometimes the sun spangles
and we feel alive.

– Simon Armitage

28
April

How wonderful it is that nobody
need wait a single moment before
starting to improve the world.

– Anna Frank

29
April

Clinging to the past is the problem.
Embracing change is the answer.

– Gloria Steinem

30
April

Be not afraid of life. Believe that life is worth living,
and your belief will help create the fact.

– William James

1

May

Imagine all the people living life
in peace.

– *John Lennon ("Imagine")*

MAY

2
May

Hope is a good thing, maybe the best
thing there is. And good things
never die.

– Stephen King

3
May

May the three aims in life be praised:
virtue, prosperity and love ...

– Vatsyayana

4

May

The importance is in your gaze,
not in the thing gazed at.

– *André Gide*

5

May

Thought makes a man great.

– *Blaise Pascal*

6

May

The only way to have a friend is to be one.

– Ralph Waldo Emerson

7

May

Happiness is like a butterfly which, when pursued, is always beyond our grasp, but, if you will sit down quietly, may alight upon you.

– Nathaniel Hawthorne

8

May

The future belongs to those who believe in the beauty of their dreams.

– Anna Eleanor Roosevelt

9

May

There is no duty we so much underrate
as the duty of being happy.

– Robert Louis Stevenson

10

May

Peace is the beauty of life. It is
sunshine. It is the smile of a child, the
love of a mother, the joy of a father,
the togetherness of a family. It is the
advancement of man, the victory of a just
cause, the triumph of truth. Peace is all
of these and more and more.

– Menachem Begin

11

May

Life is nothing without friendship.

– Quintus Ennius

12

May

Love does not have an id.

– Osho Rajneesh

13

May

The only true law is that
which leads to freedom ...

– Richard Bach

14

May

If you can't feed a hundred people,
then feed just one.

– Mother Teresa of Calcutta

15

May

Courage is the price that life exacts
for granting peace.

– Amelia Earhart

16

May

The foolish man seeks happiness in the distance;
the wise grows it under his feet.

– Julius Robert Oppenheimer

17

May

The better part of one's life
consists of his friendships.

– Abraham Lincoln

18
May

We obey our own destiny best when we
listen to our heart ...

– Uell Stanley Andersen

❧

19
May

Love is the emblem of eternity ...

– Madame de Staël

20
May

It is not in the stars to hold our destiny
but in ourselves.

– William Shakespeare

21
May

Look ahead and always aim high:
the stars aren't so far away after all!

– Paolo Nespoli

22

May

You must have chaos within you
to give birth to a dancing star.

– *Friedrich Wilhelm Nietzsche*

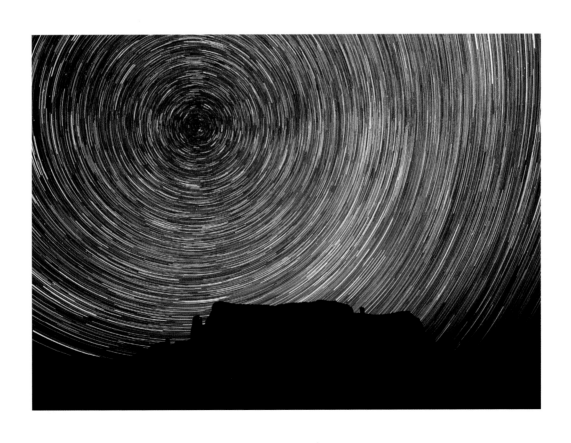

23

May

Hope is the thing with feathers
that perches in the soul
and sings the tune without words
and never stops at all.

– Emily Dickinson

🙰

24

May

Nothing is lost with peace.
Everything can be lost with war.

– Pope Pius XII

25
May

We are not asked to subscribe to any utopia or to believe in a perfect world just around the corner ... We are asked to equip ourselves with courage, hope, readiness for hard work, and to cherish large and generous ideals.

– *Emily Greene Balch*

✣

26
May

The destiny of civilized humanity depends more than ever on the moral forces it is capable of generating.

– *Albert Einstein*

27

May

The greatest love is that which friends have for one
another, because their affection is free and pure.

– Paramahansa Yogananda

28

May

He who saves one life saves the world.

– Talmud

29

May

Being myself a quiet individual,
I take it that what all men are really after is some form
or perhaps only some formula of peace.

– *Joseph Conrad*

30

May

If peace, the ideal, is to be our common destiny, then peace,
the experience, must be our common practice.

– *Henry Kissinger*

31

May

I always felt that the great high privilege, relief and comfort
of friendship was that one had to explain nothing.

– Katherine Mansfield

1

June

Real generosity towards
the future lies in giving
all to the present.

– Albert Camus

JUNE

2

June

Love is eternal - the aspect may change,
but not the essence.

– Vincent van Gogh

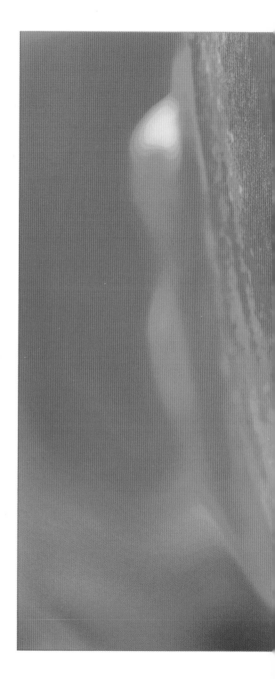

3

June

Peace is a daily
committment.

– Pope Francis

4

June

To be loved be lovable.

– Publius Ovidius Naso

5

June

Being simple and smiling is
the supreme art of the world.

– *Sergei Alexandrovich Yesenin*

6

June

A smile can add a thread
to the too short woof of life.

– *Laurence Sterne*

7

June

I am as light as a feather,
I am as happy as an angel ...

– Charles Dickens

8

June

Love conquers all.

– Publius Vergilius Maro

৵৻

9

June

... it is time to do something about peace, not just talk about peace ...

– Albert Bigelow

10

June

The world is a fine place
and worth fighting for.

– *Ernest Hemingway*

❧

11

June

Everyone on earth has a treasure
that awaits him.

– *Paulo Coelho*

12
June

It matters not how long we live, but how.

– *Philip James Bailey*

❧

13
June

... it is important not to waste human life. People cannot just be thrown away.

– *Alfred Hitchcock*

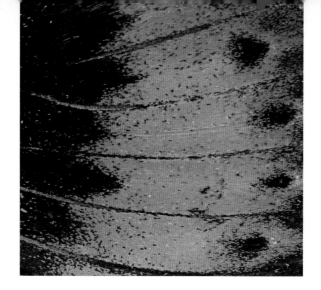

14

June

Never despise a person's sensitivity.
His sensitivity is his genius.

– Charles Baudelaire

15

June

Men, be kind to your fellow men,
this is your first duty ...

– Jean Jacques Rousseau

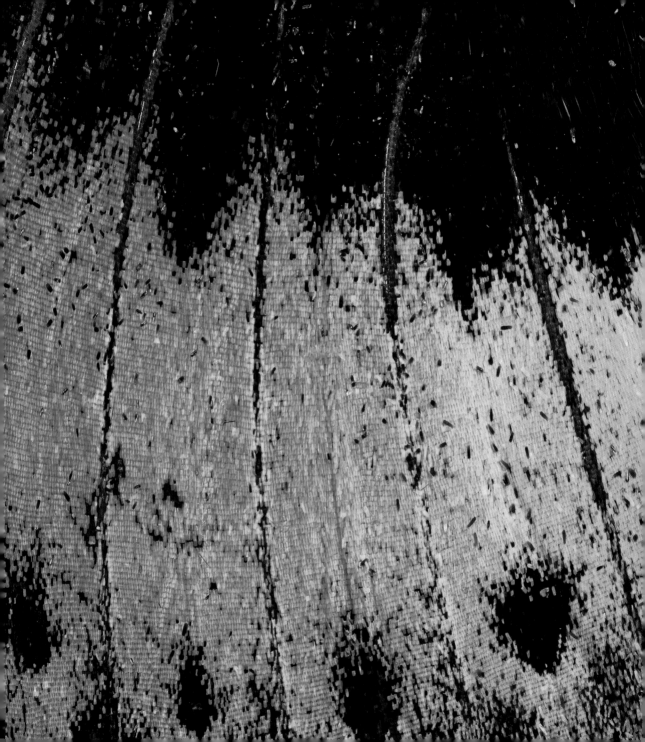

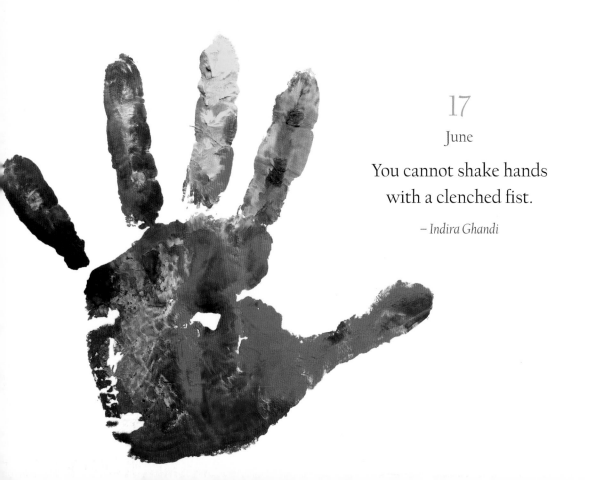

16
June

Love and art do not embrace what
is beautiful but what is made
beautiful by this embrace.

– Karl Kraus

17
June

You cannot shake hands
with a clenched fist.

– Indira Ghandi

18

June

When you realize there is nothing
lacking, the whole world belongs to you.

– Laozi

19

June

The infinite is in the human heart
and not elsewhere.

– Henry de Montherlant

20

June

Don't agonize. Organize.

– Florynce Kennedy

21

June

This is what my soul is telling me:
"Be peaceful and love everyone."

– Malala Yousafzai

If help and salvation are to come,
they can only come from children,
for children are the makers of men.

– *Maria Montessori*

23

June

The sun is new every day.

– *Heraclitus*

24

June

I have the audacity to believe that peoples
everywhere can have three meals a day for their
bodies, education and culture for their minds and
dignity, equality and freedom for their spirits.

– Martin Luther King

25

June

For me the most important thing in your life is to live your life with integrity, and not to give into peer pressure to try to be something that you're not.

– Ellen DeGeneres

26

June

Only those who are happy can give.

– Johann Wolfgang von Goethe

27

June

May love grow in your heart,
and help you to express this love
in joy and peace.

– Dorothy Day

28

June

Without peace there is nothing
truly human. Peace is harmony.
And harmony is the highest
ideal of life.

– Klas Pontus Arnoldson

29

June

I seek interior peace
by listening to myself.

– Pedro Pablo Opeka

30

June

The building of human rights will be
one of the foundation stones on which
we would build, in the world, an
atmosphere in which peace could grow.

– Anna Eleanor Roosvelt

1

July

Love is spontaneous and begs to be
able to express itself through joy,
beauty and truth.

– Leo Buscaglia

JULY

2

July

A day without a smile
is a day wasted.

– *Charlie Chaplin*

❧

3

July

All men of good will have an immense duty:
the duty to rebuild the relationship of coexistence
based on truth, on justice, on love, on freedom.

– Pope John XXIII

4

July

Peace is an irrepressible
longing in the heart
of every person, regardless
of their particular
cultural identity.

– *Pope Benedict XVI*

5

July

The measure of love is
to love without measure.

– *Saint Augustine*

6

July

Friends show their love
in times of trouble,
not in happiness.

– Euripides

7

July

Mankind must remember
that peace is not God's gift
to his creatures, it is our gift
to each other.

– Elie Wiesel

8

July

Only simplicity and truth count.
It has to come from inside. You can't fake it.

– Audrey Hepburn

❧

9

July

No medicine cures
what happiness cannot.

– Gabriel García Márquez

10

July

Your heart is greater
than your wounds.

– Henri Nouwen

11

July

No bird soars too high if he soars
with his own wings.

– William Blake

12

July

What stands if Freedom falls?

– Joseph Rudyard Kipling

13

July

Where love is,
no room is too small.

– *Talmud*

14

July

Your house is your larger body.
It grows in the sun and sleeps
in the stillness of the night; and it is not dreamless.

– Kahlil Gibran

15

July

The greatest homage we can pay
to truth, is to use it.

– James Russell Lowell

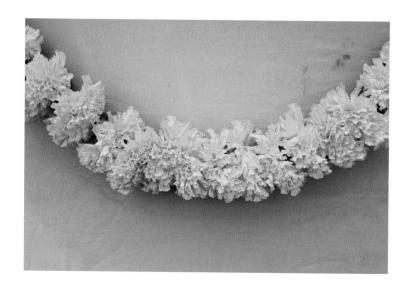

16

July

Love is, above all,
the gift of oneself.

– Jean Anouilh

17

July

May there be, in our time, at long last,
a world at peace in which we, the people,
may for once begin to make full use
of the great good that is in us.

– Ralph Bunche

18

July

To obtain what we are thinking of, we must go beyond
our limits. The result is our same limits.

– Georges Perros

19

July

Success is getting what you want.
Happiness is wanting what you got.

– Ingrid Bergman

20
July

So I urge my sisters, and my brothers,
not to be afraid. Be not afraid to
denounce injustice, though you may
be outnumbered. Be not afraid to seek
peace, even if your voice may be small.
Be not afraid to demand peace.

– Ellen Johnson Sirleaf

21
July

It is never too late to be
what you might have been.

– Mary Anne Evans (George Eliot)

22

July

After having found myself face to face
with the real problems of existence ...
I stopped fighting for trivial things
like parking spots ...

– Dominique Lapierre

23

July

Nothing can bring you peace
but yourself.

– Ralph Waldo Emerson

24
July

Peace, like freedom, is no original state
which existed from the start;
we shall have to make it,
in the truest sense of the word.

– Willy Brandt

25
July

You can't cross
the sea merely by standing
and staring at the water.

– Rabindranath Tagore

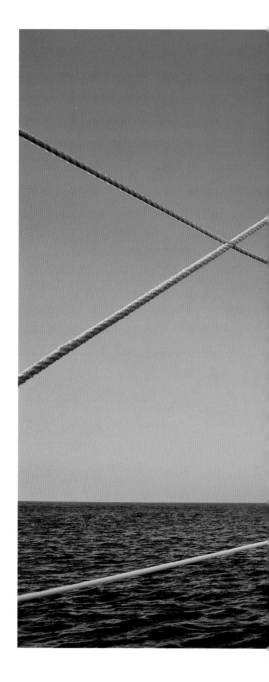

26
July

Of all our dreams today there
is no more important – or so hard to realize –
than that of peace in the world.
May we never lose our faith
in it or our resolve to do anything
that can be done to convert it one day into reality.

– Lester Bowles Pearson

27

July

We can best achieve peace by letting the peoples
of the world get to know each other better.

– Ted Turner

28

July

Do not remember the last day
and do not cry
for the tomorrow to come.

– Omar Khayyam

29

July

Heaven is to be found, neither above
nor below, neither to the right nor to
the left, heaven is to be found exactly
in the center of the bosom
of the man who has faith!

– Salvador Dalí

30
July

You have to trust in something :
your god, destiny, life, karma or whatever,
because believing that the dots will connect
down the road, will give you the confidence
to follow your heart ...

– *Steve Jobs*

31
July

It is my cherished desire that peace
be not separated from freedom,
which is the right of every nation.

– *Lech Walesa*

1

August

Love is the greatest refreshment
in life.

– Pablo Picasso

AUGUST

2

August

There is no refuge but in truth, in human intelligence,
in the unconquerable mind of man.

– Ralph Norman Angell-Lane

3

August

Blessed is the man who supports
his neighbor in his frailty ...

– Saint Francis of Assisi

4

August

My temper leads me to peace and harmony
with all men ...

– George Washington

5

August

Justice is truth in action.

– Benjamin Disraeli

6

August

... all you need is a little place in the sun and in the country, and at least the dream that there is peace on the other side of the mountain.

– Fernando Pessoa

7
August

He who has the courage
to laugh is the master of the world.

– Giacomo Leopardi

8
August

The best way to make your dreams
come true is to wake up.

– Paul Valéry

9

August

Those speeches are great not when or because
their words or phrases are great,
but when they reflect great decisions and policies.

– Ted Soresen

10

August

The true essence of peace, which ensures its
stability and durability, is justice.

– Anwar al-Sadat

11
August

The cause of peace
and the cause of truth
are of one family.

– Woodrow Wilson

12
August

Each time a man stands up for an
ideal, or acts to improve the lot
of others, or strikes out against
injustice, he sends forth a tiny ripple
of hope ...

– Robert Francis Kennedy

13

August

Fraternity is the foundation
and the way to peace.

– *Pope Francis*

14

August

The important thing is not
the amount of welfare, it is that there should be
a maximum of love among men.

– *Max Scheler*

15

August

I have a recurring fantasy that one more article
has been added to the Bill of Rights:
the right to free access to imagination.

– Azar Nafisi

16

August

When one door of happiness closes, another opens;
but often we look so long at the closed door that we do not see
the one which has been opened for us.

– *Helen Adams Keller*

17

August

Life is a wave, which in no two consecutive moments
of its existence is composed of the same particles.

– *John Tyndall*

❧

18

August

Each man had only one genuine
vocation - to find the way to himself.

– *Hermann Hesse*

19

August

Hope is a waking dream.

– Aristotle

20
August

Goodness is the only investment
that never fails.

– Henry David Thoreau

21
August

Love is the talisman of human
weal and woe ...

– Elizabeth Cady Stanton

22
August

Miracles happen
every day.

– *Deepak Chopra*

23
August

Love has no age as it is
always renewing.

– *Blaise Pascal*

24
August

Let us banish anger and hostility,
vengeance and other dark emotions,
and transform ourselves into humble
instruments of peace.

– *Carlos Filipe Ximenes Belo*

25
August

I like to believe that people in the long
run are going to do more to promote
peace than our governments.

– *Dwight David Eisenhower*

26

August

Humility is the waiting room for all perfections.

– *Marcel Aymé*

27

August

It's the little things citizens do. That's what will make
the difference. My little thing is planting trees.

– *Wangari Maathai*

28

August

Wise is the man who lives
by inventing his own illusions.

– Woody Allen

29

August

Even if happiness forgets you
a little bit, never completely
forget about it.

– Jacques Prévert

30

August

A wise man will make more opportunities than he finds.

– Francis Bacon

31

August

You can't be happy if you don't want to be.

– *Émile-Auguste Chartier (Alain)*

1

September

Learn from yesterday, live for today,
hope for tomorrow.

– Albert Einstein

SEPTEMBER

2

September

Heart is a treasure which cannot be sold
or bought, but which is given.

– Gustave Flaubert

3

September

To know how to grow old is the master work
of wisdom, and one of the most difficult
chapters in the great art of living.

– Henri-Frédéric Amiel

4
September

Force is not a remedy.

– John Bright

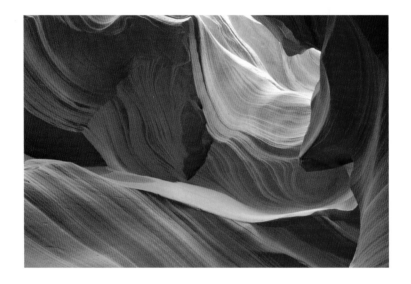

5
September

One of the eternal truths is that happiness is created
and developed in peace ...

– Bertha von Suttner

6
September

The history of the world is nothing
more than the progress of the
consciousness of freedom.

– Georg Wilhelm Friedrich Hegel

7
September

The world is rich in many peaceful
works which testify to the innate
vocation of humanity to peace.

– Pope Benedict XVI

8

September

Freedom is indivisible, and when one man is enslaved,
all are not free.

– John Fitzgerald Kennedy

9

September

Peace is not unity in similarity
but unity in diversity, in the comparison
and conciliation of differences.

– Mikhail Sergeyevich Gorbachev

10
September

I hope we can use our art
for peace and love.

– Haskell Wexler

11
September

Peace education, for example,
should be mandatory
in all schools.

– Gino Strada

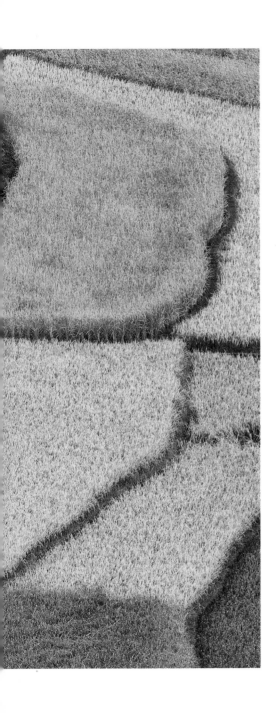

12
September

A person is a person because
he recognizes others as persons.

– Desmond Mpilo Tutu

13
September

It is possible to change the world:
all it takes is getting up, joining
with others and doing it.

– Jody Williams

14
September

... the first test of a truly great man
is his humility.

– John Ruskin

15
September

We must use time wisely
and forever realize that the time
is always ripe to do right.

– Nelson Mandela

16
September

Either peace or happiness,
let it enfold you.

– Charles Bukowski

17
September

Because I have confidence
in the power of truth
and of the spirit, I believe
in the future of mankind.

– Albert Schweitzer

18

September

One of the secrets of using
your time well is to gain
a certain ability to maintain peace
within yourself ...

– Anna Eleanor Roosevelt

19

September

The man who is serene causes no
disturbance to himself or to another.

– Epicurus

20

September

True generosity bestows more
help than advice.

– Gustave Flaubert

21

September

Man in fact does not seek a smile in the design
of happiness, but happiness in life.

– Orhan Pamuk

22

September

Dream of peace. Peace is rational and reasonable.

– Jesse Louis Jackson

23

September

It is up to each to give himself the gift of peace.

– Robert Baden-Powell

24

September

Fraternity is the only law
that makes men just.

– Henri Antoine Grouès (Abbé Pierre)

25

September

Not all that wavers falls.

– Michel de Montaigne

26

September

An honest man's
the noblest work of God.

– Alexander Pope

❦

27
September

... only dreaming and staying faithful
to dreams will we be able to be
better and, if we are better,
the world will be better.

– Luis Sepúlveda

28
September

The best way to predict the future
is to invent it.

– Alan Curtis Kay

29

September

To be able to find joy in another's joy:
that is the secret of happiness.

– *Georges Bernanos*

❧

30

September

When we can share ˗
that is the poetry in the prose of life.

– *Sigmund Freud*

1

October

You cannot hope to build a better
world without improving
the individuals.

– Marie Curie

OCTOBER

2
October

Young people, both boys and girls,
know that they must live for others
and with others, they know that their
life has meaning in that it becomes
a free gift for their neighbor.

– Pope John Paul II

3
October

Cling on like this
– I say with imagination –
to life. Like a climber around
the bars of a gate.

– Luigi Pirandello

4

October

Hope sprang eternal like
the poison mushroom.

– Charles Bukowski

5

October

My pacifism is
an instinctive feeling,
a feeling that possesses me because
the murder of people is disgusting.

– Albert Einstein

6

October

Love, whether newly born, or aroused from a death-like slumber, must always create a sunshine, filling the heart so full of radiance, that it overflows upon the outward world.

– Nathaniel Hawthorne

7

October

Unable are the loved to die,
for love is immortality.

– Emily Dickinson

8

October

Do not despair; history is not familiar
with the word 'never'.

– Willy Brandt

9

October

It seems to me that love is the most
important thing in the world.

– Hermann Hesse

10

October

Peace and justice are two sides
of the same coin.

– Dwight David Eisenhower

11

October

Love your neighbour as yourself, protect him
like the pupil of your eye.

– Jesus

12

October

The highest forms of understanding we can achieve
are laughter and human compassion.

– Richard Phillips Feynman

13

October

The universe is established according to harmony.
Friendship is also harmonious equality.

– Pythagoras

14

October

Love truth, but pardon error.

– Voltaire

15

October

We cannot look to the conscience of the world
when our own conscience is asleep.

– *Carl von Ossietzky*

❧

Act in such a way that you treat humanity, whether
in your own person or in the person of any other,
never merely as a means to an end, but always
at the same time as an end.

– Immanuel Kant

17
October

The heart has reasons that reason
does not understand.

– Jacques-Bénigne Bossuet

18
October

And so let us always meet each other with a smile,
for the smile is the beginning of love ...

– Mother Teresa of Calcutta

19

October

We have not much to say but much to share
in order to achieve by nonviolent struggle
the abolition of injustice and the attainment
of a more just and humane society for all.

– Adolfo Pérez Esquivel

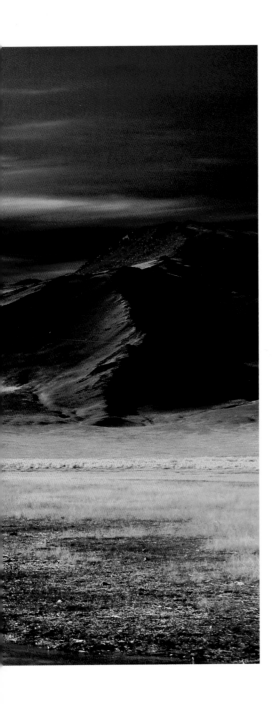

20
October

Friendship is the only cement that
will ever hold the world together.

– Thomas Woodrow Wilson

21
October

The day will never be wasted
when we have at least received
one good piece of advice.

– José Saramago

22

October

Let your instinct build a trail of wisdom,
and let your fears be diminished by hope.

– Sergio Bambarén

23

October

Even when hopeless, the struggle is still hopeful.

– Romain Rolland

The only battle that is lost
is the one that is abandoned.

– Rigoberta Menchú Tum

25

October

Life in common among people who love each
other is the ideal of happiness.

– *Amantine Aurore Lucile Dupin (George Sand)*

26

October

The man who has no imagination has no wings.

– Muhammad Ali (Cassius Marcellus Clay)

27

October

I know how men in exile
feed on dreams.

– Aeschylus

28

October

Peace is more important than all justice ...

– Martin Luther

29

October

No longer would the reign of peace be subject to the perpetual
contradictions of war, for it would rest on the unassailable bedrock
of justice, of law, and of the solidarity of peoples!

– Élie Ducommun

It is important that rulers and religious
and political leaders should realize
that there can be no peace without justice.

– Seán MacBride

31

October

Love is light, on human roads ...

– Michel Quoist

1

November

Peace is not a dram:
it can become reality. But to guard it
we must be able to dream.

– *Nelson Mandela*

NOVEMBER

2

November

Love, like medicine,
is only the art of encouraging nature.

– *Pierre-Ambroise-François Choderlos de Laclos*

3

November

The secret is to remain true to
ourselves, believe in our convictions,
be in symphony with others and
force ourselves to live that life we
have always dreamed of.

– *Sergio Bambarén*

4

November

Love, love, all the rest is nothing!

– Jean de La Fontaine

5

November

The greatest glory in living lies not in never falling,
but in rising every time we fall.

– Nelson Mandela

6

November

People need to be loved,
without love, people die.

– Diana Spencer

7

November

Spiritual peace can withstand
all of life's storms.

– Saint Pio of Pietrelcina

8
November

Freedom of expression
is the foundation of human rights,
the source of humanity,
and the mother of truth.

– Liu Xiaobo

9
November

The love is fixed,
instantly accessible to memory,
somehow stained into my body
as color into cloth.

– Anne Truitt

10
November

Compassion is the highest form of
human existence.

– Fyodor Mikhailovich Dostoyevsky

11
November

Living in charity means not seeking
your own interests but carrying the
burdens of the weaker and the poor.

– Pope Francis

12
November

A loving heart
is the truest wisdom.

– Charles Dickens

13
November

For peace is not mere absence
of war, but is a virtue that springs
from force of character ...

– Baruch Spinoza

14
November

Among things appertaining to
human life, it is friendship alone that
has the unanimous voice of all men.

– Marcus Tullius Cicero

15
November

Life is like playing a violin solo
in public and learning
the instrument as one goes on.

– Samuel Butler

16
November

I know of no greater work for humanity
than in the cause of peace, which can
only be achieved by the earnest efforts
of nations and peoples.

– Frank Billings Kellogg

17
November

I'm talking about genuine peace. The kind
of peace that makes life on Earth worth
living, and the kind that enables men and
nations to grow, and to hope, and to build
a better life for their children.

– John Fitzgerald Kennedy

18
November

Let arrival at your goal be a departure
point for a new one.

– Arturo Graf

19
November

Those who dream by day are cognizant of many things
which escape those who dream only by night.

– Edgar Allan Poe

20

November

Saving the earth does not master the earth
and does not subjugate it.

– *Martin Heidegger*

❦

21
November

It is in human nature to contain both the positive and the
negative. However it is also within human capability to
work to reinforce the positive and to minimize
or neutralize the negative.

– Aung San Suu Kyi

22

November

True love has
no knowledge of limits.

– *Sextus Propertius*

23

November

There is no path to happiness:
happiness is the path.

– Gautama Buddha

❦

24

November

All my actions have their rise
in my inalienable love of mankind.

– Mahatma Gandhi

25
November

Mistakes are to life
what shadows are to light.

– Ernst Jünger

26
November

... you don't have to push hard or
talk loud or in any way to get up to
defend what you believe in. If it is right
and if it is good and it is sound it
will defend you ...

– Frank Lloyd Wright

27
November

In the end, we will remember not
the words of our enemies,
but the silence of our friends.

– Martin Luther King

28
November

We shall not cease from exploration,
and the end of all our exploring will
be to arrive where we started and
know the place for the first time.

– Thomas Stearns Eliot

29
November

Hope is nature's veil
for hiding truth's nakedness.

– Alfred Bernhard Nobel

30
November

If we know that an obstacle
is insurmountable,
it ceases to be an obstacle and
becomes a point of departure.

– József Eötvös de Vásárosnamény

1

December

Love is like a tree: it grows by itself,
roots itself deeply in our being
and continues to flourish
over a heart in ruin.

– Victor Hugo

DECEMBER

2

December

There is no disguise which can hide
love for long where it exists,
or simulate it where it does not.

– *François de La Rochefoucauld*

3

December

The deepest love
is often hidden.

– *Yamamoto Tsunetomo*

4

December

What is it that endures when everything is changed? ...
It is love; and that alone is love, that which never becomes something else.

– Søren Kierkegaard

5

December

Friendship that flows from the heart cannot be frozen by adversity,
as the water that flows from the spring cannot congeal in winter.

– James Fenimore Cooper

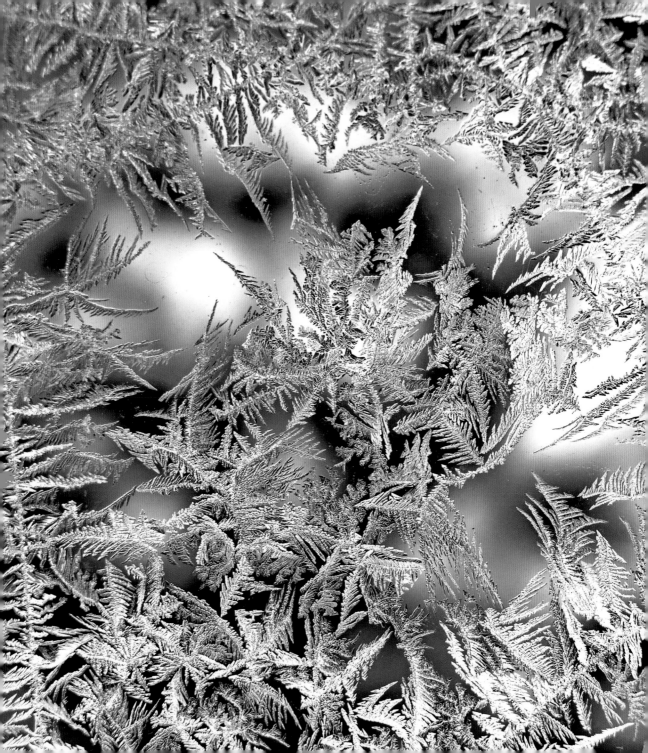

6

December

The hope and courage of a few leave indelible traces.

– Giambattista Vico

Do not go where the path may lead,
go instead where there is no path and leave a trail.

– *Ralph Waldo Emerson*

8

December

Children have no past, and that is the whole secret
of the magical innocence of their smiles.

– Milan Kundera

9

December

No man who has once heartily and wholly laughed
can be altogether irreclaimably bad.

– Thomas Carlyle

10
December

Love doesn't mean doing extraordinary or heroic things.
It means knowing how to do ordinary things with tenderness.

– Jean Vanier

11
December

Love is therefore the fundamental and innate vocation
of every human being.

– Pope John Paul II

December

Every human being, of whatever origin,
of whatever station, deserves respect.

– *Maha Thray Sithu U Thant*

13

December

Love is the only force capable of transforming
an enemy into a friend.

– Martin Luther King

14
December

Those who bring sunshine
into the lives of others cannot keep
it from themselves.

– James Matthew Barrie

15
December

... I would consider myself the
happiest of mortals if I could make
it so that men were able to cure
themselves of their prejudices.

– Montesquieu

16

December

Hope must be as limitless
as dedication.

– *Hans Urs von Balthasar*

17

December

Consider each day a life unto itself.

– *Arthur Schopenhauer*

18

December

You can't stop the waves,
but you can learn to surf them.

– Joseph Goldstein

19

December

I believe in the Law of Love.

– Clarence Seward Darrow

20

December

You shall love your neighbor as yourself.

– Jesus

21
December

The affirmation of one's own life,
happiness, growth, freedom,
is rooted in one's capacity to love.

– Erich Fromm

22

December

We must be the change
we wish to see in the world.

– Mahatma Gandhi

23

December

It is easier to recognize good than it is to define it.

– Wystan Hugh Auden

❧

How beautiful if at night each of us could say:
today I made a gesture of love
towards others.

– Pope Francis

25

December

... love is ever
the beginning
of knowledge
as fire is of light ...

– Thomas Carlyle

26
December

Peace is the hope for every man.

– Ernesto Olivero

27
December

Love is the salutation of the angels to the stars.

– Victor Hugo

28
December

The moon ages quickly. And a new moon immediately rises from the ashes of the old one.

– Kader Abdolah

29
December

Man's village
is peace of mind.

– Anwar al-Sadat

30
December

The primary asset
of any community is its dignity.

– Camillo Benso Count of Cavour

31

December

As one year has passed, so will another, and it will be
just as rich in surprises as the first one...
And so I have to go on dutifully learning...

– *Mikhail Afanasyevich Bulgakov*

LIST OF CONTRIBUTORS

A

Abdolah, Kader (Hossein Farahani), 1954-, Iranian writer (28 December)

Abiola, Hafsat, 1974-, Nigerian activist (24 March)

Adi Shankara, 788-820, Indian philosopher (22 March)

Aeschylus, 525-456 BC, Greek playwright (27 October)

Aesop, ca. 620-560 BC, Greek writer and fabulist (2 January)

Alberoni, Francesco, 1929-, Italian sociologist, journalist, and writer (11 February)

Allen, Woody (Heywood Allen), 1935-, American director, actor, and screenwriter (28 August)

Amiel-Lapeyre, Augusta (Denys Amiel), 1884-1977, French playwright (4 April)

Amiel, Herni-Frédéric, 1821-1881, Swiss philosopher and poet (3 September)

Andersen, Hans Christian, 1805-1875, Danish writer and poet (24 January)

Andersen, Uell Stanley, 1917-1986, American writer (18 May)

Annan, Kofi Atta, 1938-, Ghanaian politician, diplomat, and former Secretary General of the United Nations (6 April)

Anouilh, Jean, 1910-1987, French playwright, director, and scriptwriter (16 July)

Arias Sánchez, Óscar Rafael de Jesús, 1940-, former President of the Costa Rica (24 February)

Aristotle, ca. 384-322 BC, Greek philosopher (8 January, 19 August)

Armitage, Simon, 1963-, British poet and novelist (27 April)

Arnoldson, Klas Pontus, 1844-1916, Swedish journalist and writer (28 June)

Auden, Wystan Hugh, 1907-1973, British poet (23 December)

Aung San Suu Kyi, 1945-, Burmese politician and activist (21 November)

Aymé, Marcel, 1902-1967, French writer (26 August)

B

Bach, Richard David, 1936-, American writer (17 January, 13 May)

Bacon, Francis, 1561-1626, British philosopher, politician, and jurist (25 February, 30 August)

Baden-Powell, Robert, 1857-1941, British soldier, educator, and writer (23 September)

Bailey, Philip James, 1816-1902, British poet (12 June)

Balch, Emily Greene, 1867-1961, American writer and economist (25 May)

Balthasar, Hans Urs von, 1905-1988, Swiss clergyman and theologian (16 December)

Bambarén, Sergio, 1960-, Australian writer (31 January, 22 October, 3 November)

Barrie, James Matthew, 1860-1937, British writer (14 December)

Baudelaire, Charles Pierre, 1821-1867, French poet (18 January, 14 June)

Bayle, Pierre, 1647-1706, French philosopher, writer, and encyclopedist (18 April)

Beerbohm, Henry Maximillian, 1872-1956, British writer (10 February)

Begin, Menachem Wolfovitch, 1913-1992, Israeli politician (10 May)

Belo, Carlos Filipe Ximenes, 1948-, Catholic bishop (24 August)

Benedict XVI (Joseph Aloisius Ratzinger), 1927-, Catholic pope (4 July, 7 September)

Bergman, Ingrid, 1915-1982, Swedish actress (19 July)

Bernanos Georges, 1888-1948, French writer (29 September)

Bigelow, Albert Smith, 1906-1993, American pacifist (9 June)

Blake, William, 1757-1827, British poet and engraver (11 March, 11 July)

Bonatti, Walter, 1930-2011, Italian mountain climber (30 January)

Bond, Ruskin, 1934-, Indian writer (15 April)

Boothe Luce, Clare, 1903-1987, American journalist, politician, screenwriter, actress and diplomat (10 March)

Bossuet, Jacques-Bénigne, 1627-1704, French clergyman, theologian, and writer (17 October)

Brandt Willy (Herbert Ernst Karl Frahm), 1913-1992, German politician (24 July, 8 October)

Bridges, Robert Seymour, 1844-1930, British poet (7 January)

Bright, John, 1811-1889, British statesman (4 September)

Brontë, Charlotte, 1816-1855, British writer (13 February)

Buddha, Siddhartha Gautama, 6th century BC, Founder of Buddhism (23 November)

Bukowski, Henry Charles, 1920-1994, American poet and writer (16 September, 4 October)

Bulgakov, Mikhail Afanasyevich, 1891-1940, Russian writer and playwright (31 December)

Bunche, Raphael Johnson, 1903-1971, American political scientist and diplomat (17 July)

Buscaglia, Leo (Felice Leonardo), 1924-1998, American professor and writer (1 July)

Butler, Samuel, 1835-1902, British writer (15 November)

Byron, George Gordon Noel Byron (Lord Byron), 1788-1824, British poet and politician (14 April)

C

Cady Stanton, Elizabeth, 1815-1902, American activist (21 August)

Cameron, Julia Margaret, 1815-1879, British photographer (10 April)

Campbell, Joseph, 1904-1987, American essayist and historian of religion (14 February)

Camus, Albert, 1913-1960, French philosopher, writer, and playwright (13 March, 1 June)

Carlyle, Thomas, 1795-1881, British historian and philosopher (9 December, 25 December)

Cassin, René Samuel, 1887-1976, French jurist, judge, and diplomat (5 March)

Cavour, Camillo Benso Count of, 1810-1861, Italian politician (30 December)

Chaplin, Charlie (Charles Spencer Chaplin), 1889-1977, British actor, producer, director, and screenwriter (2 July)

Chartier, Emile-Auguste (Alain), 1868-1951, French philosopher, journalist, writer, and professor (31 August)

Choderlos de Laclos, Pierre-Ambroise-François, 1741-1803, French writer, general, and inventor (2 November)

Chopra, Deepak, 1946-, Indian physician (22 August)

Cicero, Marcus Tullius, 106-43 BC, Roman writer, attorney, and politician (31 March, 26 April, 14 November)

Coelho, Paulo, 1947-, Brazilian writer and poet (1 March, 11 June)

Coleridge, Samuel Taylor, 1772-1834, British poet, critic, and philosopher (1 April)

Conrad, Joseph (Jozef Konrad Korzeniowski), 1857-1924, Polish writer (British citizen) (29 May)

Cooper, James Fenimore, 1789-1851, American writer (5 December)

Cowper, William, 1731-1800, British poet (3 April)

Curie, Marie (Maria Sklodowska), 1867-1934, Polish chemist and physicist (French and Russian citizen) (1 October)

D

Dalí, Salvador, 1904-1989, Spanish artist (29 July)

Darrow, Clarence Seward, 1857-1938, American attorney (19 December)

Day, Dorothy, 1897-1980, American journalist and activist (27 June)

de Lamartine, Alphonse Marie Louis de Prat, 1790-1869, French poet, historian, and politician (21 January)

de Montaigne, Michel, 1533-1592, French philosopher, writer, and politician (25 September)

de Montherlant, Henry, 1896-1972, French writer and playwright (19 June)

de Saint-Exupéry, Antoine, 1900-1944, French writer and aviator (16 April)

DeGeneres, Ellen Lee, 1958-, American actress (25 June)

Democritus of Abdera, ca. 460-370 BC, Greek philosopher (25 March)

Dickens, Charles John Huffam, 1812-1870, British writer and journalist (7 June, 12 November)

Dickinson, Emily Elizabeth, 1830-1886, American poet (23 May, 7 October)

Disraeli, Benjamin, 1804-1881, British politician and writer (5 August)

Dostoyevsky, Fyodor Mikhailovich, 1821-1881, Russian writer and philosopher (27 February, 10 November)

Ducommun, Elie, 1833-1906, Swiss journalist and politician (29 October)

Dupin, Amantine Aurore Lucile (George Sand), 1804-1876, French writer and playwright (25 October)

E

Earhart, Amelia, 1897-1937, American aviator (15 May)

Einstein, Albert, 1879-1955, German-American physicist (26 May, 1 September, 5 October)

Eisenhower, Dwight David, 1890-1969, American general and thirty-fourth President of the United States (25 August, 10 October)

Eliot, Thomas Stearns, 1888-1965, American poet, essayist, and playwright (British citizen) (28 November)

Emerson, Ralph Waldo, 1803-1882, American writer, philosopher, and essayist (17 March, 6 May, 23 July, 7 December)

Ennius, Quintus, 239-169 BC, Roman poet, writer, and playwright (11 May)

Eötvös de Vásárosnamény, József, 1813-1871, Hungarian writer and politician (30 November)

Epicurus, 342-270 BC, Greek philosopher (18 March, 19 September)

Euripides, 485-407 BC, Greek playwright (6 July)

Evans, Mary Anne (George Eliot), 1819-1880, British writer (21 July)

F

Fermine, Maxence, 1968-, French writer (30 March)

Feynman, Richard, 1918-1988, American physicist (12 October)

Flaubert, Gustave, 1821-1880, French writer (2 September, 20 September)

Ford, Henry, 1863-1947, American entrepreneur (16 March)

Francis of Assisi, Saint, 1182-1226, Italian clergyman and poet (14 January, 28 March, 3 August)

Francis (Jorge Maria Bergoglio), 1936-, Catholic pope (3 June, 13 August, 11 November, 24 December)

Frank, Anna (Annelies Marie), 1929-1945, German Jew and holocaust victim (28 January, 28 April)

Franklin, Benjamin, 1706-1790, American inventor, writer, politician, and scientist (26 January)

Freud, Sigmund, 1856-1939, Austrian psychoanalyst (30 September)

Fromm, Erich Pinchas, 1900-1980, German psychoanalyst and sociologist (7 April, 21 December)

G

Gandhi, Indira Priyadarshini, 1917-1984, Indian politician (17 June)

Gandhi, Mahatma (Mohandas Karamchand), 1869-1948, Indian politician and philosopher (24 November, 22 December)

Jesus of Nazareth, 1st century AD, Founder of Christianity (11 October, 20 December)

Gibran, Khalil, 1883-1931, Lebanese-American artist, poet, writer and philosopher (12 January, 12 March, 14 July)

Gide, André, 1869-1951, French writer (4 May)

Ginzburg, Natalia, 1916-1991, Italian writer (21 April)

Goethe, Johann Wolfgang von, 1749-1832, German writer, poet, playwright, and philosopher (3 February, 26 June)

Goldstein, Joseph Leonard, 1940-, American biochemist and geneticist (18 December)

Goodall, Jane (Valerie Jane Morris-Goodall), 1934-, British ethologist and anthropologist (3 March)

Gorbachev Mikhail Sergeyevich, 1931-, Russian politician (9 September)

Gore, Al (Albert Arnold Gore), 1948-, American politician, environmentalist, and former Vice-President of the United States (1 January)

Graf, Arturo, 1848-1913, Italian poet and literary critic (18 November)

Grouès, Henri Antoine (Abbé Pierre), 1912-2007, French clergyman and politician (24 September)

Gyatso, Tenzin (Dalai Lama), 1935-, Tibetan spiritual leader and politician (11 January, 2 March)

H

Hammarskjöld, Dag Hjalmar Agne Carl, 1905-1961, Diplomat, economist, former Secretary General of the United Nations (27 January)

Hawthorne, Nathaniel, 1804-1864, American writer (7 May, 6 October)

Hegel, Georg Wilhelm Friedrich, 1770-1831, German philosopher (6 September)

Heidegger, Martin, 1889-1976, German philosopher (20 November)

Hemingway, Ernest Miller, 1899-1961, American writer and journalist (10 June)

Henley, William Ernest, 1849-1903, British poet, journalist and editor (29 March)

Hepburn, Audrey, 1929-1993, British actress (8 July)

Heraclitus, 535-475 BC, Greek philosopher (23 June)

Hesse, Hermann, 1877-1962, German writer (Swiss citizen) (22 January, 18 August, 9 October)

Hitchcock, Alfred Joseph, 1899-1980, British director and producer (13 June)

Hughes Langston, 1902-1967, American poet and playwright (10 January)

Hugo, Victor, 1802-1885, French writer, poet, politician, and activist (28/29 February, 2 April, 1 December, 27 December)

J

Jackson, Jesse Louis, 1941-, American politician, clergyman and activist (20 January, 22 September)

Jackson, Mahalia, 1911-1972, American singer (27 March)

James, William, 1842-1910, American psychologist and philosopher (30 April)

Jobs, Steve, 1955-2011, American entrepreneur and computer scientist (30 July)

John XXIII (Angelo Giuseppe Roncalli), 1881-1963, Catholic pope (3 July)

John Paul II (Karol Józef Wojtyła), 1920-2005, Catholic pope (8 April, 2 October, 11 December)

Joplin, Janis Lyn, 1943-1970, American singer (22 April)

Scott, Walter, 1771-1832, British writer and poet (23 March)

Sepúlveda, Luis, 1949-, Chilean writer, director, and activist (23 January, 27 September)

Shakespeare, William, 1564-1616, British playwright and poet (20 May)

Sirleaf, Ellen Johnson, 1938-, President of Liberia (20 July)

Soresen, Ted (Theodore), 1928-2010, Advisor to John F. Kennedy (9 August)

Spencer, Diana, 1961-1997, Princess of Wales (6 November)

Spinoza, Baruch, 1632-1677, Dutch philosopher (13 November)

Steinem, Gloria, 1934-, American journalist and activist (29 April)

Sterne Laurence, 1713-1768, British writer (6 June)

Stevenson, Robert Louis, 1850-1894, British writer (9 May)

Strada, Gino, 1948-, Italian surgeon and pacifist (11 September)

Suttner, Bertha von, 1843-1914, Austrian writer (5 September)

T

Tagore, Rabindranath, 1861-1941, Bengali poet, writer, and essayist (6 February, 25 July)

Taylor Johnson, Claudia Alta "Lady Bird", 1912-2007, First Lady of the United States (1 February)

Terzani, Tiziano, 1938-2004, Italian journalist e writer (9 April)

Thich Nhat Hanh, 1926-, Vietnamese Buddhist monk, poet, and activist (8 February, 20 February)

Thomas, Dylan Marlais, 1914-1953, British poet and playwright (19 January)

Thoreau, Henry David, 1817-1862, American philosopher, writer, and poet (15 March, 20 August)

Tolstoy, Lev Nikolayevich, 1828-1910, Russian writer and philosopher (21 March)

Truitt, Anne (Anne Dean), 1921-2004, American artist (23 April, 9 November)

Trump, Donald John, 1946-, American entrepreneur (12 February)

Turner, Ted (Robert Edward), 1938-, American entrepreneur (27 July)

Tutu, Desmond Mpilo, 1931-, South African clergyman and activist (12 September)

Tyndall, John, 1820-1893, Irish physicist (17 August)

U

U Thant, Maha Thray Sithu, 1909-1974, Burmese politician and diplomat (12 December)

V

Valéry, Ambroise Paul, 1871-1945, French writer and poet (8 August)

van Gogh, Vincent, 1853-1890, Dutch painter (2 June)

Vanier, Jean, 1928-, Canadian philosopher (10 December)

Vatsyayana, 3rd century AD, Indian philosopher (3 May)

Vico, Giambattista, 1668-1744, Italian philosopher, historian, and jurist (6 December)

Vergilius Maro, Publius, 70-19 BC, Roman poet (8 June)

Voltaire (François-Marie Arouet), 1694-1778, French writer and philosopher (4 January, 14 October)

W

Walesa, Lech, 1943-, Polish trade-union leader, politician, and activist (31 July)

Washington, George, 1732-1799, First President of the United States (4 August)

Wexler, Haskell, 1922-, American director of photography (10 September)

Whitman, Walt, 1819-1892, American poet, essayist, and journalist (29 January)

Wiesel, Elie (Eliezer), 1928-, American writer (7 July)

Wilde, Oscar, 1854-1900, Irish poet, writer, and playwright (12 April)

Williams, Berbard Arthur Owen, 1929-2003, British philosopher (3 January)

Williams, Jody, 1950-, American teacher and pacifist (13 September)

Wilson, Thomas Woodrow, 1856-1924, Twenty-eighth President of the United States (11 August, 20 October)

Winfrey, Oprah, 1954-, American anchorwoman and actress (20 March)

Wright, Frank Lloyd, 1867-1959, American architect (26 November)

X

Xiaobo, Liu, 1955-, Chinese writer and teacher (8 November)

Y

Yamamoto Tsunetomo, 1659-1721, Japanese philosopher and soldier (3 December)

Yehoshua, Abraham "Boolie", 1936-, Israeli writer (9 March)

Yesenin, Sergei Alexandrovich, 1895-1925, Russian poet (5 June)

Yogananda, Paramahansa, 1893-1952, Indian philosopher and mystic (27 May)

Yoshimoto, Banana (Mahoko), 1964-, Japanese writer (13 January)

Yourcenar, Marguerite, 1903-1987, French writer (6 March)

Yousafzai, Malala, 1997-, Pakistani student and activist (21 June)

PHOTO CREDITS

Project Editor
Valeria Manferto De Fabianis

Edited by
Gabriele Atripaldi

Graphic design
Maria Cucchi

Collaborating editor
Giorgio Ferrero

WS White Star Publishers® is a registered trademark
property of De Agostini Libri S.p.A..

© 2014 De Agostini Libri S.p.A.
Via G. da Verrazano, 15
28100 Novara, Italy
www.whitestar.it - www.deagostini.it

Translation: Alexandra Lawrence
Editing: Irina Oryshkevich

ISBN 978-88-544-0845-6
1 2 3 4 5 6   18 17 16 15 14

Printed in China